9-17-06

Birth

PLAY BY PLAY

FOOTBALL

Thanks to coaches Jerry Dunlap, Tim Mulligan, and Jack Stout, and the following Napa High School athletes who were photographed for this book:

Charlie Bahn
Thomas Barker
Jeremie Burd
Ademir Cacique
Oscar Caulderon
John Cestnik
Michael Connor
Jake DiGennaro
Ryan Dunn
Troy Eddleman
Mike Gibson
Stewart Hannah
Mario Hernandez
Grant Hubbel
Aaron Hundley
Joe LeMasters
Jesus Martinez
Iori Osawa
Masa Osawa
John Rose
Kenny Shackford
Matt Shimel
Jose Villasenor
Chris Yepson

PLAY BY PLAY

FOOTBALL

Jeff Savage

Photographs by the author

Lerner Publications Company ● Minneapolis

This book is available in two editions:
Library binding by LernerSports
Soft cover by LernerSports • FAE
Imprints of Lerner Publishing Group
241 First Avenue North
Minneapolis, MN 55401 U.S.A.

Website address: www.lernerbooks.com

Library of Congress Cataloging-in-Publication Data

Savage, Jeff, 1961–
    Play by play. Football / written and photographed by Jeff
Savage.
       p.   cm. — (Play-by-Play)
    Summary: A guide to the history, rules, skills, and
strategy of football.
    Includes index.
    ISBN: 0–8225–3935–7 (lib. bdg. : alk. paper)
    ISBN: 0–8225–0528–2 (pbk. : alk. paper)
    1. Football—Juvenile literature. [1. Football.] I. Title.
II. Series.
GV950.7.S28 2004
796.332—dc21   2002156053

Manufactured in the United States of America
1 2 3 4 5 6 – JR – 09 08 07 06 05 04

Photo Acknowledgments
Additional photographs are reproduced with the
permission of: © Bettmann/CORBIS, pp. 7, 8, 9, 10,
11; © Reuters NewMedia Inc./CORBIS, p. 18.

CONTENTS

HOW THIS GAME GOT STARTED

Football is the most popular sport in America. Baseball is still known as "America's Pastime," and soccer remains the world's most popular team game. But when polls are conducted across the United States asking people their favorite sport, football tops the list.

Why is football so popular? Because it is exciting in so many ways. Speed battles against strength. Complex plays demand cooperation and teamwork. Coaches make critical strategy decisions. The fans witness moments of sheer luck. And the color and pageantry of football makes it more than just a game. With its "tailgate" parties, cheerleaders, marching bands, and halftime shows, football contests have become events.

While football has a long history in this country, no single person invented the game. It evolved over several decades. Football began as a college game in 1867 at Princeton University in New Jersey, when a

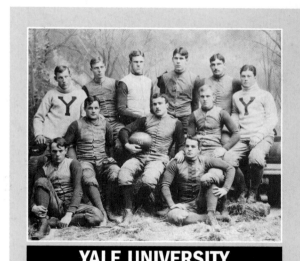

YALE UNIVERSITY

Yale players pose for a team photo, c. 1890.

A Rutgers College player makes a forward pass in a 1914 game against Princeton University.

group of young men combined the sports of soccer and rugby. Two teams of 25 players tried to kick a round rubber ball toward each other's goal line. Any player could scoop up the ball at any time and run with it. The game was called Princeton Rules. In the early 1870s, students at Harvard University in Massachusetts added variations and called their version the Boston Game. As more colleges became involved, the Intercollegiate Football Association was founded, and the first rules were written.

After 1880 a Yale player named Walter C. Camp invented many familiar features, such as the **quarterback,** the number of **downs** to advance the ball a certain distance, and a scoring system. Camp is known as the "Father of American Football." Another famous football developer is longtime University of Chicago coach Amos Alonzo Stagg. He created such features as the center **snap,** the **huddle,** and numbered jerseys.

In the sport's early years, players often wore flimsy helmets (or none at all) and little other protective gear. Not surprisingly, this became a serious problem. In 1905 the *Chicago Tribune* reported 159 critical injuries and 18 deaths from football. There was such concern that U.S. president Theodore Roosevelt demanded action. The Intercollegiate Athletic Association (IAA) was immediately founded. Rules were altered to make the game safer, such as allowing the forward pass, increasing the down distance from 5 yards to 10, and reducing the game time from 70 minutes to two 30-minute halves. Five years later, the IAA was renamed the National Collegiate Athletic Association (NCAA), and further safety measures were added.

Professional football began in 1895 with a game pitting teams from the Pennsylvania towns of Latrobe and Jeannette. Over the next 25 years, the "pros" in Pennsylvania and Ohio played each Sunday, usually for a nickel or a dime a game. In 1920 a group of men led by George Halas met in Canton, Ohio, to form the American Professional Football Association. The famous athlete Jim Thorpe was named president. Two years later, the league was renamed the National Football League (NFL). In 1960 a rival league called the American Football League (AFL) was formed. Soon, the season's winners from the two leagues met in a championship game that became the Super Bowl. In 1966 the leagues merged into the modern NFL.

As the game became more popular, high schools and grade schools added

Green Bay Packers Jim Taylor (left) and Bart Starr (center) and coach Vince Lombardi (right) concentrate on the sidelines during the 1967 Super Bowl against the Kansas City Chiefs.

programs, too. All ages could learn the same agility, strength, and skills and could run the same plays as their gridiron heroes.

This book will introduce you to the basic skills needed to play football. As with most sports, learning proper football techniques takes time and effort. Since football involves fierce contact, it is also necessary to wear the proper protective gear. If you are just starting out, you need to be supervised by an adult. Then with determination and hard work, you can become a good football player—maybe even a pro.

Chicago Bears' Gale Sayers is on his way to a 96-yard touchdown run in a 1965 game against the Minnesota Vikings.

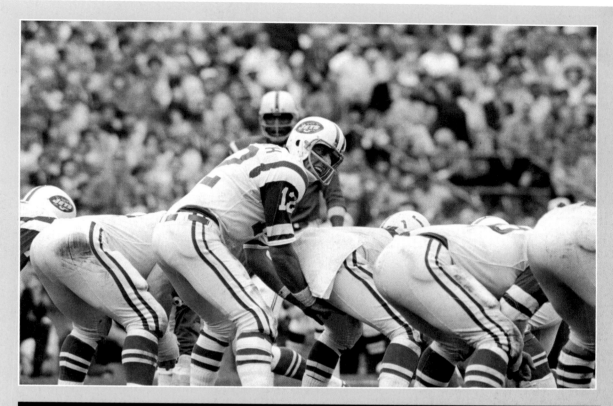

THE SUPER BOWL

Each year the NFL season ends with its championship game: the Super Bowl. This game is usually the most-watched television show of the year. Advertisers pay millions of dollars just to air a 30-second commercial. The halftime show on the field often features spectacular fireworks and the most popular musicians in the world.

The first Super Bowl was played January 15, 1967, at the Los Angeles Memorial Coliseum. But it was not called the Super Bowl then. It was dubbed the AFL-NFL World Championship Game. The Green Bay Packers, led by legendary coach Vince Lombardi, defeated the Kansas City Chiefs, 35–10. A year later, Lombardi's Packers won the title again, beating the Oakland Raiders, 33–14.

In 1969 the name was changed to "Super Bowl," and the practice of using Roman numerals for each year's game began. At Super Bowl III, quarterback Joe Namath (above) of the AFL's champion team, New York Jets, "guaranteed" victory over the heavily favored NFL's Baltimore Colts. Namath's Jets shocked the nation by winning, 16–7.

Over the years, at least 15 teams (about half the teams in the NFL) have won the Super Bowl. The San Francisco 49ers and the Dallas Cowboys have won the most—five Super Bowls each. With the victory comes the Vince Lombardi Trophy and a grand parade witnessed by thousands of fans in the champion's home city.

BASICS

Football is played between two teams that try to score points by moving a football up the field and across a goal line for a **touchdown.** The football can be moved either by throwing it to a teammate or by **running** with it. Points are also scored by kicking the football between two goalposts or by tackling an opponent in possession of the ball in his **end zone.**

The game is divided into four quarters. In pro and college football, each quarter lasts 15 minutes. In high school football, each quarter lasts 12 minutes. The side with the most points at the end of the game is the winner.

FIELD OF PLAY

Football is played on a field of grass, or occasionally artificial turf, 100 yards long and 53⅓ yards wide. Lines extending the width of the field are spaced 5 yards apart. Between each 5-yard line are short lines, called hash marks, that indicate each yard. The center of the field is marked by the 50-yard line, which is also called the midfield stripe.

At both ends of the field is the widest line, called the goal line. Extending 10 yards deeper is the last line, called the end line. The area between the goal line and the end line is the end zone. Four plastic or foam rubber pylons, usually orange, are placed in each end zone to mark the inbound corners. On each end line is a goal made up of a crossbar and two upright goalposts. The crossbar is 10 feet off the ground. The uprights range from 18 feet 6 inches apart in high school football to 23 feet 4 inches apart in the pros.

Finally, running the length of the field—120 yards including both end zones—are the sidelines. Action beyond the sidelines is out of bounds.

EQUIPMENT

A football uniform is designed to reduce the risk of injury. You should not play tackle football without wearing a full uniform.

The helmet is the most important piece of equipment worn by football players. Its shell is made of a very hard plastic called Kevlar, the same

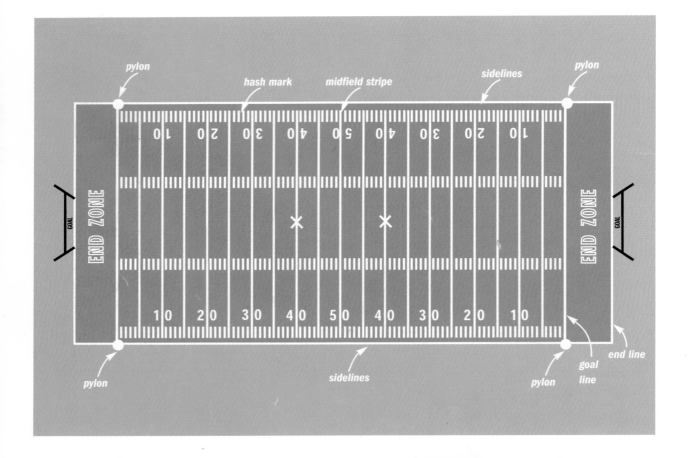

material used in police body armor. The inside of the helmet is lined with foam or inflatable padding. Attached to the front of the helmet is a face mask made of several thin, plastic-covered metal bars.

Shoulder pads are also made of plastic and lined with padding. These pads extend across the shoulders and chest to protect against body blows. Joints and other sensitive areas are covered by knee pads, thigh pads, hip pads, mouth guards, and protective cups. These are all required gear. Optional pads include elbow pads, forearm pads, shin pads, and neck rolls.

Jerseys feature the player's uniform number on the front and back, and sometimes on the shoulders. The player's name appears on the back in the pros and often in college football. Pants are made of a tight-fitting elastic material with pockets inside to hold the knee and thigh pads. The tight, smooth material also makes it hard for opponents to grab. Shoes have rubber or plastic cleats to dig into the turf, giving players solid footing.

BALLS

Footballs have a unique shape, oval with pointed tips. The shape is also called a spheroid. A football is about 11 inches long and between 27 and 28 inches in circumference at the widest point. Weighing about 14 ounces, a football is inflated to a pressure of between 12 and 14 pounds per square inch. High school footballs have a white stripe encircling either end. College footballs have the same white stripes, but they only go around half the ball. Pro footballs do not have white stripes.

Footballs range in price, depending on their brand and material. The best footballs are made of leather with string laces similar to shoelaces. Balls made of rubber with plastic or rubber laces are also available. Some of the earliest footballs were made from pigs' skin. You may often still hear a football referred to as "the pigskin" or a game referred to as a "pigskin classic."

BASIC MOVES

In California the Napa High School varsity football team practices basic skills every day. The most important techniques the team members learn are **passing,** catching, running, **blocking,** and defending. These basic skills are put into play in every game, either in trying to score **(offense)** or trying to prevent the other team from scoring **(defense).**

PASSING

A team's offense can advance the football in two ways, by passing or running (also called rushing). Passing can be highly effective if performed properly, but it is also more dangerous than running. It is often said that when a ball is passed, three things can happen, and two of them are bad. The best outcome is a **completion,** where the ball is caught by a teammate. But if the ball is dropped or otherwise not caught, it is an **incompletion,** which is not good. And definitely not good is an **interception.** That's when the other team catches the ball. With those odds, passing the ball well is critical to a team's success in moving it.

To pass well, the thrower must hold the football properly. This is called the grip. Joe holds the ball with his fingers across its laces. The ideal motion of

the ball in flight is a smooth rotation called a spiral. Joe puts his fingers over the laces for a secure grip, giving him more control of the ball's motion as he throws it. He spreads his fingers wide for even more control.

Before throwing the pass, it is important to keep both hands on the football. Only when you are about to release the ball should you be holding it one-handed. In making the pass, stand up tall, step forward with the foot opposite your throwing hand, and follow through. Joe throws with his right hand, so he steps forward with his left foot as he is about to deliver. He reaches back and then propels his entire upper body forward and around, thereby using more muscles to deliver a crisp pass. The angle of his arm as he comes through is not directly over his head, nor at the side, but somewhere in between. This is often referred to as the three-quarter angle.

CATCHING

For a pass to be successful, it needs to be caught by a teammate. Sounds simple, but it is not easy to catch a spiraling (or wobbly) football while running at full speed with opponents chasing you.

The most critical element in catching is concentration. The key to concentrating is to "look" the football all the way into your hands. Your fear of

getting hit by opponents will tempt you to turn and look to see where they are. If you do, though, you are likely to drop the ball. And the irony is, you are probably going to get hit anyway.

The main technique in catching is to use two hands. Certainly some passes are barely within reach. In these cases, you should do whatever it takes with one hand to keep the ball from touching the ground. Otherwise, always use two hands to catch the ball. And catch the ball *with* your hands and not your body.

Aaron demonstrates how to catch a pass over his head. He reaches up high with both hands. As the ball arrives, he never takes his eyes off it. He grabs the ball with both hands and squeezes it. Then he pulls the ball toward his body where he will protect it.

QUARTERBACK!

Peyton Manning (number 18) is one of the best quarterbacks in the NFL. He grew up in Louisiana, where his father, Archie, was the quarterback of the New Orleans Saints. Peyton grew up surrounded by football, and he always knew he wanted to be a quarterback like his father. He reached that dream through hard work and persistence.

Even as a toddler, Peyton was playing Nerf football at home. As Peyton grew older, he and his brothers often went to see Saints' games. The boys got to play on the field at halftime and go into the locker room after games. Peyton got a real taste for the sport.

His turn as a star quarterback in high school earned him a college scholarship to the University of Tennessee. At Tennessee, he spent most of his waking hours studying—his schoolwork and the football playbook. In 1998 he was the very first player drafted in the NFL, by the Indianapolis Colts.

Peyton surprised the Colts coaches by how hard he worked. Each day before practice, he spent several hours in the film room studying opposing defenses. After practice he stayed on the field alone to run sprints. He set NFL rookie records for completions, yards, and touchdowns. By his second season, the Colts were in the playoffs, and Peyton was an All-Pro (the best NFL player at his position).

RUNNING

Running on a football field is not easy. Cleats provide traction, but the grass still might be slippery or a recent rain could make the field muddy. You are also wearing 10 pounds of gear and a helmet that impairs your field of vision.

You should run as you normally do when sprinting or running straight. But when changing direction, lower your body more than normal to compensate for the extra weight you are carrying and for the condition of the field. This is called a crouch.

If you are running with the ball, a good way to escape a tackle is to use a **fake.** By lunging your body in one direction, you lure your opponent into moving that way, too. Then you abruptly change direction by planting your foot and shifting your weight. The key to avoiding injury is this simple rule: the faster the speed or the sharper the cut, the deeper the crouch to make.

BLOCKING

Teams cannot advance the football without solid blocking, usually from the offensive line. Wherever the ball goes, several defenders are usually in close pursuit. Blocking is the technique used to protect a teammate in possession of the ball.

LINGO

There are many special terms for plays, players, errors, and efforts. Watching and playing the game is probably the best way to learn those terms and how they're applied. But here is some basic lingo commonly used in every game.

- **audible:** a last-minute change of plans shouted by the quarterback to his team at the **line of scrimmage,** just before the play starts. Also called an automatic.
- **blitz:** a play in which the defense sends secondary players rushing across the line of scrimmage as soon as the ball is snapped to try to sack the quarterback
- **bomb:** a long pass thrown to a receiver sprinting down the field
- **clipping:** an illegal block from behind and often below the waist. Clipping is a personal foul (one that could cause injury) punishable by a 15-yard **penalty.**
- **drive:** the series of plays a team puts together in its attempt to score
- **fumble:** the ball carrier losing **possession** by dropping the ball or having it knocked away before a play ends
- **rush:** to run from the line of scrimmage with the ball or to run toward the quarterback for a tackle
- **sack:** the tackle of a quarterback behind the line of scrimmage. A sack results in a loss of yards for the offense.

John Cestnik (left), Michael Connor (right), and their teammates practice blocking every day. John and Michael demonstrate the form used in making a proper block. John, on offense, is the blocker. Michael is the defender. John drives forward with his legs toward Michael. He engages Michael with his arms and upper body.

John keeps his head up! Smart players are careful to always keep their head up whenever they make contact with an opponent. You can lower your head as long as the rest of your body goes with it. But never lower your head so much that your chin touches your chest. And never purposely make contact with an opponent with the top of your helmet. Even with protective gear, impact at that angle could cause a serious neck injury.

As John makes contact, he keeps his hands in front of him and between Michael's shoulder pads. This is called keeping your hands inside. John would commit a penalty by wrapping his arms around Michael. He makes contact with Michael and then sustains the block (keeps it going). John drives forward with his legs, pushing up and into Michael for as long as necessary. Michael, meanwhile, will try to escape from John. Called shedding the block, this can be done with footwork or by shoving John to one side. Shedding a solid block requires strength and quickness.

DEFENSE

A team's defensive side is on the field when the team does not have the ball. A team cannot succeed without a solid defense. This includes **guarding** and **tackling,** but of the two, the first defensive skill is tackling.

TACKLING

To demonstrate a proper tackle, Michael and John reverse roles. Michael, playing defense, charges forward from a low angle. As he arrives in front of John (on offense), he bends his knees more to get even lower. He reaches around John's frame to grab him with both arms. This is called wrapping up. Unlike with blocking, this move is not penalized in tackling.

Michael keeps his head up! Remember, a smart player always keeps his head up when making contact with an opponent.

Maintaining his hold on John, Michael keeps his momentum moving forward by pumping his legs. He keeps his back straight as he moves forward and up, lifting John into the air. Then he lowers the weight of his body into John and drives him into the ground. As John is about to be tackled on his back, he tries to put his chin to his chest. This is the only instance in which you should do this. John is trying to prevent his head from banging on the ground.

GUARDING

Only the player in possession of the football may be tackled. Players not in possession of the ball are either blocking or trying to get free to receive a pass. Defenders are either trying to shed blocks or guarding those attempting to get free for a pass. When guarding, a defender is not permitted to make contact with an opponent until the opponent touches the ball.

Each offensive player has at least one defensive player guarding him. To guard his man, at the start of the play, the defender can stand any-where he wants on his side of the line of scrimmage (where the ball will be snapped). If the defender is guarding a swift player, he should play several steps away from, or "off," the offensive player. This is the position that Troy assumes as he guards John Rose (facing page). This stance also applies when a defender knows he will not get help from another teammate behind him.

If, however, the defender knows he can get help from a teammate from behind, he could play up, or "tight," on his opponent. This is the position Tommy takes as he guards Aaron (wearing jersey number 80). With the play **in motion,** the defender wants to stay as close to his opponent as possible without

touching him. This gives him an excellent chance at batting away a pass or intercepting it.

Defender Tommy guards "tight" against opponent Aaron (number 80).

Defensive player Troy plays "off" John Rose (number 81).

Chapter 3

GAME TIME

POSITIONS

In the game of football, there are 11 players on the field for each team. As we learned earlier, the team with the football is on offense. The team without the ball is the defense.

In a standard formation on offense, the **center** snaps the football back between his legs to the quarterback and then blocks. The left guard and right guard line up on either side of the center to block. The left tackle and right tackle line up next to the guards to block. The **tight end** lines up next to either tackle. Depending on the play, his role is either to block or catch passes. These six players together are called the offensive line.

The two **wide receivers** line up on either side of the offensive line to run downfield and to catch a pass. The quarterback lines up behind the center to receive the snap. The quarterback can pass the ball, hand it off, or run with it himself. The **fullback** lines up three yards behind the quarterback

to take a handoff and run with the ball, go out for a pass, or block. The **tailback** lines up three yards behind the fullback to take a handoff and run with the ball, go out for a pass, or block.

In a standard formation on defense, the two defensive tackles line up facing the two offensive guards. The two **defensive ends** line up facing the two offensive tackles. These four players together are called the defensive line. Their job is to rush (try to tackle) the quarterback on pass plays and to tackle the ball carrier on run plays. The **linebackers** line up three yards behind the defensive line. The two outside linebackers line up on either side of the middle linebacker. Their job is to rush the quarterback, tackle the ball carrier, and guard players who might be going out for a pass. The two **safeties** line up several yards behind the linebackers. They are the last line of defense. Their job is to tackle a ball carrier who breaks through the defensive line and to guard players who run downfield for passes. The two **cornerbacks** line up in front of the two wide receivers. Their job is to guard the receivers and prevent them from catching passes and to make tackles when they can.

RULES

A touchdown is scored when any part of the ball crosses the goal line while in the possession of a player before he is tackled. A touchdown is 6 points. The ball is then placed on the 2-yard line, and the team that scored the touchdown can attempt either an **extra point** or a **2-point conversion.** One point is scored if the team kicks the ball between the uprights. Two points are scored if the team advances the ball into the end zone by passing or running.

During a possession, a team may be close to the goal line but have only one more down to play. The offense

WHAT IT'S WORTH

Touchdown	6 points
Point after touchdown conversion (PAT), kicking	1 point
Point after touchdown conversion (PAT), on the ground	2 points
Field goal	3 points
Safety	2 points

may choose to use the last down to kick a **field goal** to get the points. A field goal is scored when the offense kicks the ball between the uprights. A field goal is 3 points.

A **safety** is scored by the defense when an offensive player possessing the ball is tackled in his own end zone. A safety is 2 points.

The game begins with a coin toss to determine which team will kick off. The ball is kicked off from the 30-yard line in pro football and the 35-yard line in college and high school football. The receiving team attempts to return the football as far upfield as possible.

Before each play, a game **official** places the ball at a spot on the field. This is the line of scrimmage. The offense gathers in a huddle where the quarterback gives them instructions for the play. He tells the team how it will block, who will get the ball, and when the center will snap the ball to him. Sometimes the offense can be directed without a huddle, in which case the quarterback yells the play to his teammates at the line of scrimmage. The defense tries to identify the play and react as quickly as possible.

The offense has 4 downs (plays) to gain at least 10 yards. If it does so on any of the 4 downs, it becomes first down again with another 10 yards to go. Scoring terms reflect this, as in first and ten (first down with 10 yards

to go), second and five, and so on.

If the offense fails to advance the ball 10 yards, it forfeits possession to the other team. On fourth down, the offense has three options. It can try to advance the ball past the first-down marker. It can attempt a field goal for 3 points. Or it can **punt** the ball to the defense. A kick of any sort is an automatic forfeiture of possession.

A player in possession of the ball is considered down when a defensive player causes any portion of that player's body, except for hands and feet, to touch the ground.

At that point, an official blows a whistle, and play stops. A player is also down at the point where he goes out of bounds.

GAME PLAN

Coaches are responsible for making the decisions in a football game. There are at least four and as many as eight coaches on a team. The head coach is in charge. The assistant coaches help with certain groups of players. Together they are called the coaching staff.

A primary job of the coaching staff is to devise a game plan. Coaches must consider the strengths and weaknesses of their team and compare them to the strengths and weaknesses of their opponent. They must think of ways their offense can score and ways their defense can stop the opponent. Then they must write down their ideas on paper.

Such ideas are drawn in the form of diagrams and charts. The offensive players are marked in an alignment on one side of the line of scrimmage while the defense is drawn on the other side. The standard code is to use an "X" for each defensive player and an "O" for each offensive player. Lines are drawn to depict where each of the Xs and Os (players) are supposed to go on the play.

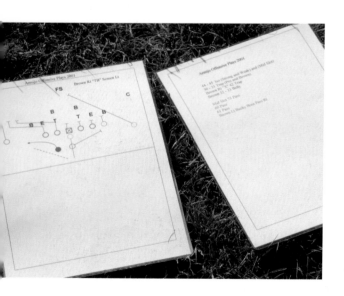

FOULS

The **referee** (head official) and his team of officials decide when the rules have been broken. There are more than 30 rule violations, with penalties ranging from a loss of 5 yards to a loss of 15 yards or more.

Minor violations of the rules include illegal motion or being off-side. Offensive players must pause, or be "set," for one second before the ball is snapped. Illegal motion occurs when an offensive player moves after the set position but before the ball is snapped. A defensive player is offside when he crosses the line of scrim-mage before the ball is snapped. Illegal motion and offside each carry a penalty of 5 yards.

Other violations include holding, roughing, facemask, and pass inter-ference. Holding can be committed by the offense or the defense. A player cannot grab another player with his hands or arms and hang on. Holding is a 10-yard penalty. Roughing occurs when a player is aggressive beyond the limits allowed. Roughing includes delivering an unnecessary blow to an opponent's head or hitting an oppo-nent after the whistle is blown to stop play. Quarterbacks and kickers are especially protected against roughing. Such a penalty costs a team 15 yards. A facemask penalty occurs when a player grabs another by the face mask, jerking the player's neck. A facemask penalty can be either 5 or 15 yards, depending on whether the player touched the face mask or pulled on it. Pass interference occurs when a player interferes with his opponent's ability to catch the ball beyond the limits allowed. This includes bumping or grabbing the opponent while the ball is in the air. If the defense commits the penalty, the ball is placed at the site of the infraction, and the offense is awarded a first down. If the offense is at fault, it is penalized 10 yards.

PLAYING THE GAME

The Napa High varsity football team is preparing for its first game of the season. At each of its practices, Coach Dunlap pits the offense against the defense in a series of plays from the line of scrimmage. Coach Dunlap directs the offense. Coaches Mulligan and Stout instruct the defense.

The offense huddles eight yards behind the line of scrimmage. Joe at quarterback announces the play: "Pro left, 31 trap, on two." The players break the huddle by clapping once and shouting "Score!" They take their positions at the line. Michael and Iori line up as running backs behind Joe. Masa and Aaron split wide as receivers. Oscar, Chris, Ryan (the center), Jake, and Stewart are the linemen. Troy is the tight end on the left.

"Down!" Joe barks. "Set! Hut . . . Hut!"

Ryan snaps the ball to Joe, who turns to hand it off to Michael. Shoulder pads pop as the offensive linemen smack into the defenders. Michael runs through the line and into the defense where he is tackled

by Kenny and Jeremie. The coaches blow whistles to stop the action.

"Good job, line!" says Chris.

Coach Dunlap applauds. "Nice block, Oscar."

The ball is returned to its original spot. In a practice, the team is not interested in marking off the yardage gained on a play. These repetitions ensure that the players are working together as a team.

Ryan stands eight yards behind the ball and raises his arm. "Huddle up!" he yells. The players gather around and lean in to listen to Joe. "Spread right, 35 option, on down," he says. The players break the huddle and take their stances. "Down!" Joe yells, and Ryan quickly snaps the ball. Joe runs left with it. The defense pursues that way with him. Kenny breaks through the line and comes at Joe. At the last instant, Joe pitches the ball to Iori, who gathers it in and bursts into the teeth of the defense. Linebackers Charlie and Grant converge to make the tackle.

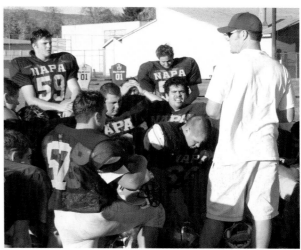

The players get up and trudge back to the huddle.

"Gentlemen, huddle up!" yells coach Mulligan. "I said this was live! Move it!"

The players spring to attention and hurry back for the next play.

"Doubles left, 70s cross, on one," says Joe. At the line, he takes the snap and drops back to pass. Defensive linemen Mike and Jose grunt as they drive hard with their legs to rush the quarterback. Masa and Aaron are covered downfield when suddenly they cut at the same time in opposite directions. Joe steps up and fires a pass. It's perfect. Aaron pulls it in with two hands before he is tackled by Ademir.

"Hey, that's a great double team," says Coach Dunlap to Jake and Stewart. "And that was a nice throw, Joe."

The water girls run among the defenders with plastic bottles. Players quickly take gulps before the offense breaks its huddle.

"C'mon, defense!" shouts Jeremie.

The offense comes to the line of scrimmage, and the defenders get set to make a stop. "Louie! Louie!" shouts Charlie to tell his teammates that the offense has more players lined up on the left side of the ball. (He'd shout "Roger, Roger!" if there were more to the right.) The defense shifts slightly to the left side. Joe hands the ball to Michael, who heads left and then cuts upfield. John Rose, the safety, makes the stop. "Attaway, 81!" Coach Stout yells to John. Teammates pat John on the helmet.

"Second O!" Coach Dunlap calls out to indicate the offense's substitutes should take the field. "Second O, let's go!"

The substitutes hurry onto the field. Jesus moves in at quarterback. "Spread right, 15 speed option, on two," he says. Jesus leads the team to the line.

"Don't just walk up to the ball!"

Coach Mulligan yells. "You guys don't hustle, we're gonna run in full gear from 5 o'clock to 6 o'clock, how would you like that?!"

The players urge one another to hustle up. The next several plays are crisp.

The scrimmage continues for an hour. Pads pop and whistles blow as the offense runs all manner of plays, such as sweeps, end arounds, options, and reverses. The defense tries differ-ent formations like man-to-man and zone with extra linebackers and defensive backs. When that ends, players take a short break to catch their breath and drink water. But practice is not yet over.

TIME OUT

FIRST DOWN

DELAY OF GAME

LOSS OF DOWN

TOUCHDOWN

**INCOMPLETE
FORWARD PASS**

OFFICIALS

Officials are in charge of the game. They spot the ball (place it on the field for play) and enforce the rules. Their decisions are final. There are at least four officials for a high school game, five for college, and seven for pro. Officials wear white pants, black-and-white striped shirts, and black caps (except for the referee who wears a white cap). They carry a whistle to blow to stop play.

The referee is the boss. He controls the game and announces the penalties. The umpire is responsible for action along the line of scrimmage, such as holding. The head linesman watches for offside and helps deter-mine where the ball is spotted after each play. The line judge helps the head linesman and also times the game. There is usually a clock on the stadium scoreboard, but the official time is kept by the line judge on his wrist-watch. The back judge watches for holding and infractions involving the quarterback. He also monitors the 40-second clock. When the ball is spotted for play, the offense has 40 seconds to snap the ball again, or it will be penalized 5 yards for delay of game. The side judge marks where players go out of bounds with the ball. The field judge scans the field for holding and other penalties.

IT'S NOT ALL PHYSICAL

Vince Lombardi led the Green Bay Packers to five NFL championships. He's often called the greatest coach of all time. Many of his quotes are famous, especially those concerning determination and a winning mentality.

It's not whether you get knocked down. It's whether you get up again.

Winning isn't everything, but wanting to win is.

Individual commitment to a group effort— that is what makes a team work, a company work, a society work, a civilization work.

TWO-WAY PLAYER

Pro and college football players concentrate on one position. In high school, however, some players are so valuable to their team that they play both offense and defense. This is called "playing on both sides of the ball" or "going both ways." A player who does this is called a **two-way player.**

Players are permitted by rules to play any position they like. But two-way players most often play positions on both sides of the ball that fit their skills. For instance, offensive linemen are usually big and strong. On defense, they would best be suited to play on the line again, as either a defensive end or a tackle. Wide receivers generally are swift and have sure hands. A natural defensive position for them would be at cornerback or safety.

Some exceptional athletes play more than both ways. They also serve on **special teams.** They might block on the offensive line for punts and kicks or they might be the punt and kick returner. The quarterback is often the **holder** on extra points and field goals.

Chapter 4

PRACTICE, PRACTICE

When the Napa High team is not scrimmaging with its offense and defense, the players are improving their skills by conducting **drills.** These drills are both fun and exhausting.

CONDITIONING

Before the players begin drills, they must warm up properly. The warm-up routine helps prevent injuries. Players begin by jogging in place to get their blood flowing. Next, they stretch their muscles to improve flexibility. Proper stretching is critical in any sport, but it is especially so in football, where the players are running and making awkward maneuvers while wearing heavy gear.

Troy, John Cestnik, and the rest of the players help one another to stretch leg muscles or tendons such as hamstrings. The players perform other stretching exercises, such as crossovers, or "pull-it-to," in which they pull their right leg over their left and hold it, and then switch to left over right.

DRILLS

The Napa High team begins its drills by practicing **stances.** Starting from the proper point is important in executing a play from any position. With his fellow linemen watching, Ryan demonstrates the proper technique for a 3-point stance (below). It is so called because Ryan is touching the ground at three points, with two feet and one hand. Chris shows the correct form for a 4-point stance (top right). At the snap of the ball, Chris will look up so that any contact his head makes with his opponent will be with the front of his helmet and not the top (crown).

Next, Jose and the rest of his teammates form a line. At the sound of a coach's whistle, they will spring from their stances and run several yards. Finally, the offensive and defensive lines practice in unison, under the watchful eye of Coach Mulligan. The coach checks their positioning and looks for the slightest flinch. When the players are blasting out of their stances together as a unit, Coach Mulligan will end the drill for the day, only to do it again tomorrow.

Meanwhile, Joe is working with his **skill-position** teammates on their stances. The quarterback, wide receivers, and running backs are the so-called "skill" positions on a team. This does not mean that they have more skill than other players, just that they handle the ball more. With Coach Dunlap observing, Joe simulates taking snaps from center. The instant the play starts, the fullback surges forward from his 3-point stance and the tailback moves from his 2-point stance (standing upright with knees bent).

Foot skills are important in football. One of the trickiest drills is the **running ropes.** Aaron leads the way and Ademir follows as they demonstrate how to step quickly through the ropes. They step with their left foot into a right square, then step with their right foot into a left square, and so on. These are called crossovers. Such footwork loosens up ligaments and tendons in the legs.

Several drills are performed using the **bags.** Coach Mulligan watches the players demonstrate the bag run. This drill improves agility and teaches players to run with their knees high. Tackles and blocks are often made at the ankles. Players who run with "high knees" can step out of such tackles and blocks.

A second bag drill is the bag run combined with the blocking bags. Players run with high knees over the bags, then turn and hit the blocking bags. This simulates game action in which a player might be dodging through traffic and then making a downfield block.

Yet another bag drill is the bag jump. Players improve their vertical jump by performing this drill. As their legs become more powerful, they are able to jump over more bags. Coach Dunlap likes to test his best players by stacking several bags.

One drill especially for offensive linemen is the **chutes.** Players start in a set position. At the sound of the coach's whistle, they fire out through the chutes while staying low. This drill teaches offensive linemen to stay low as they block on a running play. The most effective blocks are those in which the lineman is like a battering ram, leading with the front of his helmet and shoulder pads. It is difficult for a defender to shed such a block.

A popular drill is the **7-man sled.** All offensive and defensive linemen work with the sled, as do other defenders such as linebackers and safeties. The sled weighs several hundred pounds, so it is difficult to move.

At the sound of the whistle, seven players hit the sled and begin driving forward with legs churning. This drill obviously strengthens thigh and calf muscles. But it also tests a player's determination and encourages teammates to work together. When the players hit the sled hard enough at the same time, the sled will raise up off the ground just enough so that the players can drive it farther. The coaches might split the players into three groups of seven and challenge each group to push the sled farther.

A drill that combines several others is blocking and tackling. The players can take what they learn from such drills as stances, chutes, and the 7-man sled and apply these techniques to actual blocking and tackling. Coaches create various combinations to simulate game situations. One offensive lineman will try to block one defensive lineman. This is called "one-on-one." Two offensive linemen will block one defensive lineman (below).

This is called a "double team." Coaches keep a watchful eye on these drills to ensure players use proper form.

The players have scrimmaged and performed drills, and practice is nearing an end. It is time for the most grueling drill of all: **sprints.** Sprinting helps make the players faster and builds up their endurance. The coaches demand a certain number of sprints and distances, depending on how practice went that day. If the players practiced hard and well, the sprints will be few. If practice did not go smoothly, the coaches will demand numerous sprints.

For each sprint, all the players line up on the field, side by side in a set stance. Coach Mulligan announces the distance for that sprint, say, 15 yards. He blows his whistle, and the players spring forward and race to the 15-yard line, touch it with their hand, and sprint back to the starting line. Some sprints may be shorter, some longer. Coach Mulligan might have the players run 20 sprints or more. Any time the coach sees a player who is not running hard, he demands that sprint to be run again. The players groan but know they have to run hard or they could be out there all night! The players are exhausted at the end of the sprints. Some drink water. Others search for air to breathe. A few collapse on the ground to rest.

Chapter 5

SPECIAL TEAMS

Offense and defense are equally important units of a football team. But a third unit is often overlooked: special teams. The Napa High coaches and players understand the value of special teams. That is why they work hard on all aspects of special teams play.

Special teams are groups of players used in certain situations. A special teams situation arises more than once every five plays. On average, more than 20 percent of a game is played by a special teams unit. Each team has six special teams units. They are the kickoff team and kickoff return team, the punt team and punt return team, and the field goal team and field goal defense team. A player may play on any number of these special teams units. Some offensive or defensive players also serve on special teams units.

WATER!!!

Eating is not allowed during football practice. But there is one thing you should take in throughout practice: water! This is known as hydration.

In one hour of a typical practice, a player can sweat out as much as a quart of perspiration. Those fluids have to be replenished. Just as the earth is mostly water, so are we, including 75 percent of our muscle tissue. If a player does not get enough water, he can suffer from a sudden, painful, involuntary muscle contraction, better known as a cramp. The body also struggles to control its own temperature during exercise, and water helps that, too. Luckily, this all-purpose liquid is cheap and easy to find. So stay hydrated!

KICKOFFS

A game starts with a special teams play—a kickoff. The ball is placed on a kicking tee at the 30-yard line in a pro game (35-yard line for college and high school) of the team that is kicking off. Eleven players line up behind the line of scrimmage and run forward as one of them, the **kicker,** boots the ball downfield. The kick return team usually positions two kick returners near its goal line. One of them often fields the ball—either by catching it or scooping it up off the grass— and then runs upfield with it. His teammates block for him as he tries to gain as much yardage as possible before being tackled by the kickoff team. Any member of the kickoff return team may field the ball and advance it. If the ball is kicked 10 yards or more and is not yet touched, it is considered a "live" ball, and either side may gain possession of it. A kickoff also starts the second half of the game and follows every score.

FIELD GOALS

When the offensive team is faced with a fourth-down situation on its opponents' side of the field, it can stay on the field to try to gain a first down, punt the ball to the opponent, or attempt a field goal. (A field goal can be attempted on any down, but the best strategy is to wait until fourth down.) A field goal is successful if the ball is kicked over the crossbar between the uprights.

The field goal team is comprised of a **snapper,** a holder, a kicker, and eight linemen who try to prevent defenders from blocking the kick. The field goal team is also the extra point team. The defensive team is generally

a collection of players who can rush hard or jump high to try to block the kick. If a kick is blocked, the ball is "live," and the defense can advance it. The offense is then cast in a defensive mode and must try to recover the ball or stop the defense from advancing it. On longer field goal attempts, the defender positions a player deep near the end zone. If the ball is taken in the field of play, it can be returned, like a kickoff.

Sometimes a field goal might be needed to win the game. The Napa High team practices regularly on field goal attempts. Jesus, Joe, and Matt demonstrate the proper technique in kicking a field goal. Jesus is the long snapper. Joe is the holder (also called a spotter). Matt is the kicker. Joe is positioned on his knee seven yards behind the line of scrimmage. Matt stands several steps behind Joe and to one side. Jesus hikes the ball with one hand on a low spiral to Joe. Jesus then helps his teammates block. Joe places the ball on the ground on its end and holds it with the tip of his index finger. If Joe has time, he turns the ball so that the laces are aiming forward. Matt strides forward to kick the ball. Matt kicks with his right foot. His left foot is called his plant foot. Matt plants his left foot slightly ahead of the ball. He sweeps his right leg through and kicks the ball with the instep of his foot toward the goalpost.

PUNTS

On fourth down, the offense may attempt to gain a first down by running or passing the ball. If the attempt fails, the ball is placed at the spot where the player in possession is tackled, and the opponent takes possession there. Rather than go for a first down, the offense may elect to surrender possession by pushing the other team as far back as possible with a punt.

The punt team is comprised of a snapper, a **punter**, and nine players who have dual roles. On the first part of the play, they try to prevent defenders from blocking the punt. On the second part, they try to tackle the player in possession of the ball.

The punt return team is made up of a punt returner and 10 players who also have dual roles. On the first part of the play, they try to block the punt. On the second part, they block for their teammate who is in possession of the ball. The players with dual roles are taught to listen for the thump of the punt.

After the ball is punted, the first phase of the play is over, and the second phase begins. The punt returner fields the ball and tries to gain as much yardage as possible before being tackled by the punt team. Any member of the punt return team may field the ball and advance it.

If the ball is not touched by a member of the return team, it may be downed by any player on the punt team at the spot where he first touches it. If the ball goes into or through the end zone, it is spotted at the punt return team's 20-yard line. If the punt goes out of bounds, it is spotted where it crossed the sideline into out-of-bounds territory. Finally, if the players hear a thump-thump, they know the punt has been blocked. If the punt is blocked, the ball is "live," and the defense can advance it.

Punting is important in terms of field position (where teams take possession of the ball). The Napa High team regularly practices punting and covering punts.

Jesus and Matt (facing page) demonstrate the proper technique in punting. Jesus is the long snapper. Matt is the punter. Matt stands about 10 yards behind the line of scrimmage. Jesus snaps the ball with one hand directly to Matt in a low spiral. Jesus then helps his teammates block.

Matt catches the ball and holds it out in front of him with two hands. If he has time, he turns the ball so that the laces are up. He strides forward and drops the ball as he steps into the punt. He kicks the ball with the top of his foot. He follows through with his kicking leg until his foot is as high as his helmet.

REACHING YOUR GOAL

There are two steps to becoming a good football player. First, you must learn proper techniques. In this book, the Napa High football team demonstrates these basic skills for you. Second, you must practice these techniques. The Napa football players practice every day. They repeat the same moves over and over again. They understand that it takes hard work to be the best. If you are willing to learn and practice, you are on your way. You may even become the next football star.

FOOTBALL TALK

bags: Heavy pads used in practice for drills. Players jump over bags and practice blocking into them.

blocking: The technique used to protect a teammate in possession of the ball as defenders try to tackle him.

center: A player on the offensive line. On each play, the center snaps the ball to the quarterback and then helps block defenders.

chutes: A large metal device about four feet high used in practice drills. Offensive linemen stay low as they run through the chute.

completion: A catch of a pass beyond the line of scrimmage. Also called a reception.

cornerback: A defensive player lined up opposite a wide receiver. The cornerback's job is to guard the receiver and prevent him from catching a pass. Cornerbacks also tackle when they can.

defense: The team of 11 players not in possession of the football. The defense tries to prevent its opponent from advancing the ball and scoring.

defensive end: A player on the defensive line of scrimmage. The two defensive ends line up facing the two offensive tackles and rush the quarterback on pass plays and tackle the ball carrier on run plays.

down: A unit of play that begins with the snap of the ball and ends when the whistle blows. A down is also a play.

drills: Basic movements performed by players in practice designed to improve skills.

end zone: The area measuring 10 yards in length beyond the goal line. Teams try to advance the ball to this area.

extra point: After a touchdown, the single point scored by the offense when the kicker successfully kicks the ball over the crossbar and between the uprights.

fake: A movement by a player in which he lunges his body in one direction to lure the opponent that way, then abruptly changes direction to try to get past the opponent.

field goal: A successful kick over the crossbar and between the uprights. The offense can attempt a field goal on any down and from any distance. A field goal is 3 points.

fullback: A player who lines up 3 yards behind the quarterback to take a handoff and run with the ball, go out for a pass, or block.

guard: 1) A player position, mainly used for blocking. The left guard and right guard line up on either side of the center on the offensive line. 2) A technique used by a defensive player to prevent an opponent from catching a pass.

holder: On plays for field goals and extra points, the player who receives the snap from center and places the ball on the ground for the kicker. Also called a spotter.

huddle: A brief gathering of players on the field, away from the line of scrimmage. Players receive their instructions for the next down during the huddle.

incompletion: A pass beyond the line of scrimmage that is not caught, resulting in a loss of down.

in motion: A player in motion runs parallel to the line of scrimmage or away from it. Only one offensive player is permitted to move before the ball is snapped. Also called man-in-motion.

interception: A pass that is caught by a defensive player, resulting in a change of possession.

kicker: A player who kicks the ball on kickoffs and for field goals and extra points.

linebacker: A player lined up about 3 yards behind the defensive line. The three linebackers rush the quarterback, tackle the ball carrier, and guard players going out for passes.

line of scrimmage: An imaginary line across the field, originating from the nose of the football after it is spotted for play. The offense and defense stay on opposite sides of the line and cannot cross it until the ball is snapped.

offense: The team of 11 players in possession of the football. The offense tries to advance the ball down the field to score points.

officials: The men on the field who are in charge of the game. They spot the ball and enforce the rules.

passing: One of two ways the offense can advance the ball. A play is considered a pass if it is thrown across the line of scrimmage. Any offensive player may attempt a pass.

penalty: A violation of a rule, imposed by the officials. A penalty accepted by the opponent may result in the loss of down, yardage, or both.

possession: In control of the football. The offense is usually in possession. When the defense gains possession, its offensive teammates take the field to control the ball.

punter: A player 10 yards behind the center who catches a snap and kicks it, or **punts,** before it hits the ground.

quarterback: A player in charge of directing the offense. The quarterback announces the play in the huddle, calls signals at the line of scrimmage, receives the snap from the center, and then passes the ball, hands it off, or runs with it.

referee: The head official. The referee controls the game and supervises the other officials.

running: One of two ways the offense can advance the ball. A play is considered a run if any player attempts to carry it across the line of scrimmage.

running ropes: A practice drill designed to improve footwork. Players step quickly through a web of thin ropes about one foot off the ground.

safety: 1) A defensive player lined up several yards behind the linebackers. The two safeties are the last line of defense. Their job is to tackle ball carriers who break through the defensive line and to guard players who run downfield for passes.
2) A score by the defense when an offensive player possessing the ball is tackled in his own end zone. A safety is 2 points.

7-man sled: A large device constructed of metal and pads that seven players attempt to push forward by churning hard with their legs.

skill position: A player who routinely handles the ball more than players in other positions.

snap: To quickly hand the ball between the legs to a player standing directly behind. A center usually snaps the ball to a quarterback to begin each play.

snapper: A member of a field goal team, responsible for hiking the ball between the legs to the holder.

special teams: The units of 11 players that play on kickoffs, field goal attempts, extra-point attempts, and punts.

sprints: A drill in which players line up side by side in a set stance, run quickly to a predetermined spot, and run back to the starting point.

stance: The position a player assumes to execute a play.

tackle: 1) An offensive player position, mainly used for blocking. The left tackle and right tackle line up next to the left guard and right guard on the offensive line. 2) A player position on the defensive line. The two defensive tackles line up in the middle at the line of scrimmage to rush the passer or stop the ball carrier. 3) A technique in which a player stops a ball carrier by causing any portion of that player's body, except for hands and feet, to touch the ground.

tailback: A player who lines up three yards behind the fullback to take a handoff and run with the ball, go out for a pass, or block.

tight end: An offensive player who lines up next to either offensive tackle to block or catch passes.

touchdown: A score in which the offense moves the ball into the opponents' end zone. A touchdown is 6 points.

2-point conversion: After the touchdown, the two points scored by the offense when it successfully runs or completes a pass into the end zone from the 2-yard line.

two-way player: A player who plays on both the offense and defense.

wide receiver: An offensive player position, mainly used for big gains. Wide receivers line up on either side of the offensive line to run downfield and catch passes from the quarterback.

FURTHER READING

Barber, Phil. *NFL's Greatest: Pro Football's Best Players, Teams, and Games*. London: DK Publishing, 2000.

Italia, Bob. *100 Unforgettable Moments in Pro Football*. Edina, MN: Abdo & Daughters, 1998.

Savage, Jeff. *Peyton Manning: Precision Passer*. Minneapolis, MN: LernerSports, 2001.

FOR MORE INFORMATION

National Collegiate Athletic Association (NCAA)
P.O. Box 6222
Indianapolis, IN 46206
<http://www.ncaafootball.net>

National Football League (NFL)
280 Park Avenue
New York, NY 10017
<http//www.NFL.com>

NFL High School Football
<http://www.nflhs.com>

INDEX

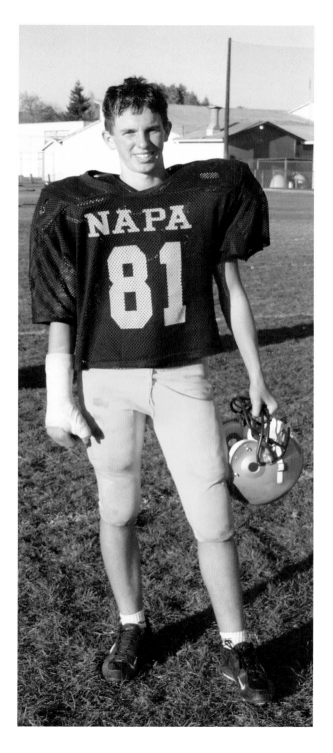

ABOUT THE AUTHOR

Jeff Savage is the author of more than 120 sports books, including LernerSports' *Fundamental Strength Training*. He lives with his wife, Nancy, and sons, Taylor and Bailey, in Napa, California. For this book, he profiled the local Napa High School football team. Many outstanding athletes have starred for Napa High through the years. Still, Jeff believes that Taylor and Bailey will one day star at quarterback and wide receiver for Napa High and shatter all passing and receiving records as they lead the team to the state championship.